My Emotions Through Emojis

FEELING EMBARRASSED

BY
THEIA LAKE

Enslow
PUBLISHING

T0019607

Please visit our website, www.enslow.com.
For a free color catalog of all our high-quality books, call toll free
1-800-398-2504 or fax 1-877-980-4454.

Cataloging-in-Publication Data
Names: Lake, Theia.
Title: Feeling embarrassed / Theia Lake.
Description: New York : Enslow Publishing, 2024. | Series: My emotions through emojis | Includes index.
Identifiers: ISBN 9781978533332 (pbk.) | ISBN 9781978533349 (library bound) | ISBN 9781978533356 (ebook)
Subjects: LCSH: Embarrassment in children–Juvenile literature. | Embarrassment–Juvenile literature. | Self-consciousness (Sensitivity)–Juvenile literature. | Emotions–Juvenile literature.
Classification: LCC BF723.E44 L35 2023 | DDC 152.4–dc23

Published in 2024 by
Enslow Publishing
2544 Clinton Street
Buffalo, NY 14224

Copyright © 2024 Enslow Publishing

Designer: Tanya Dellaccio Keeney
Editor: Theresa Emminizer

Photo credits: Cover (phone) Victor Z/Shutterstock.com; cover, series art (clouds) Theus/Shutterstock.com; cover, series art (emojis) stas11/Shutterstock.com; p. 5 Roquillo Tebar/Shutterstock.com; pp. 7, 11 Krakenimages.com/Shutterstock.com; p. 9 Harbachova Yuliya/Shutterstock.com; p. 13 imtmphoto/Shutterstock.com; pp. 15, 17 fizkes/Shutterstock.com; p. 19 ANURAK PONGPATIMET/Shutterstock.com; p. 21 stockfour/Shutterstock.com.

All rights reserved. No part of this book may be reproduced in any form without permission in writing from the publisher, except by a reviewer.

Printed in the United States of America

Some of the images in this book illustrate individuals who are models. The depictions do not imply actual situations or events.

CPSIA compliance information: Batch #CS24ENS: For further information contact Enslow Publishing, at 1-800-398-2504.

Find us on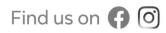

CONTENTS

Boldface words appear in Words to Know.

ARE YOU EMBARRASSED?

Have you ever felt embarrassed? Embarrassment means feeling **uncomfortable**. When you're embarrassed, you might want to hide your face. You might have a tight feeling in your stomach.

Feeling embarrassed isn't fun. But you aren't alone! Everybody feels embarrassed sometimes.

HOW EMBARRASSING!

On Tuesdays, Cal played basketball. It was his favorite part of the week 😁!

But one day at practice, Cal reached for the ball and his gym shorts ripped. The other kids laughed. Cal felt his face get hot 😳. How embarrassing!

ACCIDENTS HAPPEN

We usually feel embarrassed when we do something silly or have an **accident** of some kind.

Embarrassment can make us feel very alone. It helps to remember that embarrassing things happen to everybody! Life can be messy. Accidents happen every day!

9

LAUGH IT OFF!

Cal wanted to run out of the gym. He felt a **lump** rising in his throat. He wanted to cry 😥.

Cal closed his eyes. He took a deep breath 😣. He looked at his friends' smiling faces. Cal started laughing too 😆!

TELL SOMEBODY

Sometimes when we're embarrassed, we don't feel like laughing it off. If someone laughs at us, it can really hurt our feelings!

If you're too embarrassed to laugh it off, it can help to share your feelings with someone you trust.

A BAD FEELING

Ani had always been proud of her hair 😄. But lately, something changed. A girl at school had been **teasing** Ani about her hair.

The teasing embarrassed Ani 😕. It made her want to stay home from school. Ani felt sick 🤢.

15

LET IT OUT!

Ani's mom asked her what was wrong. At first, Ani didn't want to tell her about the girl 😶. But the longer she kept it inside, the sicker she felt 😑.

Ani decided to talk to her mom. Just saying it out loud helped a lot!

FIND WHAT HELPS

Can you think of other things that make you feel better when you're unhappy?

Maybe you have a pet at home you could cuddle with. Or a favorite book you like to read. Writing about your feelings is great too!

FEEL YOUR FEELINGS

Feeling embarrassed can be hard. But you aren't alone! It happens to everyone.

Feelings come and feelings go. When you're embarrassed, know it will pass! You can cry if you want to. You can laugh too! Don't be afraid to feel how you feel.

21

WORDS TO KNOW

accident: An unexpected event that happens by chance.

lump: A bump or something that sticks out.

teasing: Picking on someone or laughing at them in a mean way.

uncomfortable: To feel uneasy.

FOR MORE INFORMATION

BOOKS

Bromage, Fran. *I Can Feel*. New York, NY: Windmill Books, 2022.

Harasymiw, Therese. *Are You Being Bullied?* New York, NY: PowerKids Press, 2021.

WEBSITES

Kids Health
kidshealth.org/en/kids/talk-feelings.html
Learn how to name and talk about your feelings.

Stop Bullying
www.stopbullying.gov/cyberbullying/how-to-deal-with-haters
Learn how to deal with difficult people and feelings.

Publisher's note to educators and parents: Our editors have carefully reviewed these websites to ensure that they are suitable for students. Many websites change frequently, however, and we cannot guarantee that a site's future contents will continue to meet our high standards of quality and educational value. Be advised that students should be closely supervised whenever they access the internet.

INDEX

24